How to Behave in the **House of God**
(The Case Against Casual Worship)

Pastor Robert L. Dickie
Berean Baptist Church

Berean Baptist Church
6705 Rustic Ridge Trail
Grand Blanc, MI 48439
www.allgrace.com

www.emmausroadpress.com

Copyright © 2018 by Robert L. Dickie

All rights reserved. No part of this book may be reproduced, scanned, or distributed in any printed or electronic form without permission.

Cover Design and Editorial Design: Jerry Carter Jr.

Frist Edition: March 2018

Printed in the United States of America
ISBN: 978-0-9964998-7-3

Table of Contents

Preface _____ 1

Introduction _____ 5

1 What Does Scripture Have
To Say About Casual Worship? _____ 15

2 What Does Tradition Have
To Say About Casual Worship? _____ 43

3 What Does Common Sense Have
To Say About Casual Worship? _____ 55

4 What Does Cultural Compromise Have
To Say About Casual Worship? _____ 61

Conclusion _____ 69

Preface

At the outset of this study on casual dress in worship, I want to make it clear that I have a deep love for the people of God. I love God's church and long for her purity, effectiveness, blessing, and protection. I have been a preacher of the gospel for over 50 years. I have spent 45 years of my life pastoring Christian churches. I have spent the past 36 years in my present church. Over the years, I have preached all over the world to crowds of people ranging from 16,000 in India to over 25,000 in St. Louis, Missouri. At my present church, we have enjoyed times of unusual blessing where many came to faith in Christ, and we have also known times of sadness and sorrow. In all of these times, I have remained convinced that whatever happens in our ministries, we need to give all the glory to God for His aid and divine help. Praise God from Whom all blessings flow.

I am not expressing my conviction on casual dress out of jealousy of the successes and blessings of other pastors. I have always taught that true success in the ministry is being faithful to God and in proclaiming the whole counsel of His Word. Through the years I have seen fads, false doctrines, and movements come and go. What alarms me now is the adoption of casual worship that seems to have swept across all of

Christendom in the West. I pray that what I have to say in these pages will not come across as judgmental or condescending to those with whom I differ. I do not wish to cause any division or confusion for any church leaders or pastors, nor do I desire to enter into endless debates with those who wish to argue a different opinion. If you read these pages and do not agree with me, you do not need to worry about what I think. We need to be concerned with what the God of the universe thinks about our beliefs and actions. At the end of the day, we each answer to the Lord. I do, however, ask you to pray about what I am saying here. I would ask you to avoid making a quick emotional response. I am asking that you read this carefully, slowly, and prayerfully and see if the Lord does not speak to your heart. Hear what I have to say on this subject of casual worship in the house of the Lord. Weigh all the evidence that I am going to share with you.

I am writing on behalf of many ministers who, like me, are dismayed at what they see in the churches across our land. I have seen young ministers who preach at enormously large churches, dress down, appear casual and cool, while at the same time bring excellent messages. Does this justify how they dress? The answer is no. I believe the impact of their ministry would be deeper and richer if they gave serious thought as to what they are wearing in the pulpit and what it is saying about them, about their God, and about what the world thinks of them. In the Old Testament, God not only required His priests to dress appropriately; He also made sure their priestly garments were designed in such a way to ensure their dignity and respect.

To teach that ministers and the Lord's people should dress appropriately for worship is not a popular thing to do. One person's casual clothes may be another person's dress up clothes. I am suggesting that pastors give this subject of how they dress in the pulpit and in church prayerful reflection. We all want our churches to be filled with the glory of God. We desire that our services will be characterized by the reverent spirit of God's presence. Let us pray that the Lord will guide His people and give each pastor wisdom in leading his church in corporate worship in such a way that will not distract from the glory of God or hinder the message of the gospel. If all I accomplish here is to cause the Lord's people to rethink this subject, I trust it will be of some benefit to the glory of God in His church.

Introduction

"But if I tarry long, that thou mayest know how thou oughtest to behave thyself in the house of God, which is the church of the living God, the pillar and ground of the truth."   I Timothy 3:15

Ours is a generation that is so focused on self and obsessed with meeting felt needs that it can hardly see the relevance of the Apostle's statement in I Timothy 3:15. Why would this generation of church goers give much thought to such a statement? If today's worshippers are focused on "my wants," "my needs," "my happiness," "my comfort," why would they pause to reflect on what the God of the Bible requires of them when they gather in His presence? For the most part, there is only a superficial concern being shown to how we should worship God and the corollary of how we should dress when we come into the presence of God.

This is a day in which pastors should teach their parishioners how they should behave and dress in the house of God. Far too many of today's professing Christians come to church flippantly and irreverently. Few come to church well-prepared by prayer, meditation and by having spent time in God's presence preparing their soul to worship God and to receive His Word.

The great Welsh preacher of the 18th century, Daniel Rowlands, commented on how the people in the Welsh valleys gathered for church on the Lord' Day. That was a time of great preaching when powerful gospel messages exhorted, proclaimed the riches of Gods grace, exalted Christ, convicted men of sin, and brought down the presence of God to their congregations. Rowlands saw many of these common people walk great distances to hear the Word of God proclaimed. As he saw these people coming down the mountains and passing through the valley's they were all singing praise to God as they came. Daniel Rowlands said, *"Here come the Lord's people— bringing God with them."*

Today's generation cannot appreciate the deep significance of those words. You cannot bring God with you to church, (in this sense) unless you have first met with Him and have spent time in His presence.

We need to teach our youth and our adult congregations, once again, the importance of reverence to God, respect to the Lord's house, and to those who preach the gospel. We need to teach them that we draw near to worship the Most High in a spirit that is not only filled with joy and praise but is also characterized by the fear of God.

If ministers want their parishioners to see them as their buddy and as one whom they consider just one of the "good ole boys," then they should dress causal, dress down, dress cool, dress like they have just come from a ball game or picnic. But if ministers desire their people to respect their biblical authority, consider the pulpit a sacred place where God meets with their pastor to feed and guide them, then they should dress in a manner that demonstrates that they understand the deep significance of standing in the presence of God.

Introduction

Casual dress for ministers in the pulpit is grossly inconsistent with the minister's holy calling and his position in the pulpit as a man who stands between heaven and hell.

In the Christian church, God's people have always understood that how we worship God is of profound importance. There is among the various segments of Christendom great debates, discussions, and differences of opinions on how we should worship God. While other religions also have debates on how to worship, it seems that nothing has been comparable to the worship wars and confusion that is found within the Christian church. The question that I'm asking in this study is this, *"Does casual dress in our worship services by both the ministers and the laity, enhance or detract from biblical worship?"* I believe casual dress detracts from the worship of God.

To support my answer, I want to appeal to four different sources of evidence that speak either directly or indirectly to this subject. The four areas of discussion will include, scripture, tradition, common sense, and cultural compromise with worldliness.

I admit that I have personal preferences on this subject. Our answer to the question *"Does casual dress in our worship services by both the ministers and the laity, enhance or detract from biblical worship?"* must not be based on our prejudices and personal preferences. First and foremost, we must be convinced and guided by the Word of God. Only after we have sought counsel from the Scriptures can we make appeals to church traditions, common sense and cultural compromise. But none of these other areas of argument can in any way conflict with the Word of God.

The subject of casual dress in worship must not be confused with the trivializing of Christian worship by unbiblical innovations. While casual dress is a part of the problem of trivializing Christian worship it also stands alone as its own concern. A church might maintain proper forms for worship while allowing for casual dress in the worship service.

To make people feel more comfortable in church, many pastors are now wearing jeans, sport shirts, T-shirts, shorts, and other types of casual clothing when they preach. Many young pastors, and even some older ones as well, will be heard to say, *"You can come to our church dressed any way you like. We have no dress standards here."* Is this really a biblical thing to say? Does this kind of thing help reach the unchurched? One Christian leader spoke directly to this subject and made a good case for rejecting casual dress for worship:

> *"I've always heard it explained that the purpose of casual dress in the church is to reach people and relate to them on their level. That sounds noble enough on the surface (and I'm all for reaching the lost), but follow that logic just a little deeper and there are big spiritual problems that are hard to reconcile. To start with, casual dress gives the impression that the things of God are neither serious nor holy. Those of us who are aware that people's eternal destinies are at stake should consider the ministry of Christ too important to treat casually.*
>
> *Many might argue that the reason they do dress down is because they are so concerned about the lost. I don't doubt their sincerity, but again, the logic just doesn't make sense. If I need a medical specialist, I am not turned off if he or she is dressed more formally than I. If I need a policeman, I don't mind that he's dressed up in a uniform.*

Introduction

When receiving help from these professionals, it is actually a comfort to see them dressed in a way that shows they understand the importance of their place. I don't need a person wearing what I am wearing just so he or she can relate to me. Why should the preacher or saint in a worship setting have to look like the sinner in order to reach them? I know Christians are trying to send the message, "Hey, we are all just like you," but that is not our message, nor is it true. The sinner is not one of us, and the Holy Spirit is working throughout the service to show him that, so that when the opportunity is presented, he will become one of us. When we gear our worship exclusively toward the comfort of sinners (the popular but less scriptural phrase in our day is the un-churched), we are actually working against the convicting ministry of the Spirit. Let's work on making God comfortable in our services, and we will have maximum effectiveness in preaching and demonstrating the good news of the love of Christ to the sinner." [1]

Is it possible that we are compromising biblical standards to accommodate the world in which we live? I believe we are. I'm not addressing the content of our worship, the style of music, the place where we gather or the liturgy or lack of one. I'm just focusing on how we as pastors dress when we minister at church and what we expect when we open the doors for the Lord's people to come and worship as well. I have been a pastor for well over 40 years. I have seen many trends come and go. I have also seen the collapse of western civilization and the departure of the glory of God from most of the West including the United States. In our desperate attempts to address the free fall of the church, the departure of God's blessing, and the encroachment of many false religions in our land, I have seen many ministers resort to new measures and ideas to try and reverse the church's descent into insignificance. So far, with all these new ideas, new theologies, and new philosophies on how to do church, I have not seen anything that has really worked. The crisis of a fading Christianity in the West has not been halted. One observer of the current trends in worship commented on what he saw as people came to church:

> *"They saunter into church in baggy shorts, flip-flop sandals, tennis shoes and grubby T-shirts. Some even slide into the pews carrying coffee in plastic foam containers as if they're going to Starbucks. "It's like some people decided to stop mowing the lawn and then decided to come to church," "No one dresses up for church anymore."* [2]

Those who promote and defend casual dress in worship will often cite that those who believe in dressing appropriately for worship are legalistic and judgmental to those who come to church casually. I have not found this to be true. I don't know anyone who would be unkind to someone who came to church dressed in casual clothing. I have never heard of any pastor or church turning people away from the service because they were not dressed according to the expectations of the church.

I believe that ministers who have adopted casual dress for worship have not helped the overall health or spirituality of the church. In fact, it is my contention that this trend, although well-intentioned, has hurt the Christian cause more than it has helped.

The church of the late 20th century and the first part of the 21st century will be widely known as a church that was casual, careless, compromised, comfortable, content, and carnal. When future generations look back on this period of church history, they may well list among their main critiques of the church of this era, that it lacked a godly leadership that had the spiritual ability to discern between the holy and the profane.

Pastors who dress down on the Lord's Day and parishioners who follow suit may seem like an insignificant issue in the light of so many other pressing concerns. However, this trend of casual dress in worship is a symptom of much deeper concerns. At the root of this popular trend are the following concerns:

1. Lack of discernment
2. Compromise with worldliness
3. Failure to recognize the real need of the sinner, which is regeneration, not a watered-down version of Christianity and worship to entice him to come to church
4. Failure to rely on the power of the Holy Spirit
5. Failure to teach people how to behave in the house of God
6. Absence of the fear of God in our spiritual lives and churches
7. And finally, a defective understanding of ecclesiology. (This means that those who dress down for worship have a view of the church that sees worship as being casual. They fail to see that worship is ritualistic, liturgical, and highly formal. They also assume that because we are under the New Covenant, we can do just about anything we want.)

The real problem is not that dressing casual is sinful, it's not. The real problem is to be able to discern that there is a time and a place to be casual. The worship service is not one of them. A Christian leader commented on casual dress for worship:

> *"It is the habit of my family to dress for church. I have, on more than one occasion, argued in print that we casually worship a casual god because we enter into his presence casually. I have suggested that on the Lord's Day we should dress as if we were going to meet the King, because we are going to meet the King. I know, from experience, that it won't take long for someone to point out the obvious, that God looks not at the outward, but at the heart."* [3]

I am not advocating for any specific dress codes for pastors and people. In the various Christian denominations, there have always been standards of dress that were considered appropriate for ministers and laity alike. The orthodox priests have worn various types of religious garments that set them apart for their work and ministry. In many reformed churches, the clergy have worn clerical robes. In most evangelical and independent churches a coat and tie or shirt and tie were considered respectful dress for the worship service. I am not suggesting a strict dress code that should be enforced by church officers. I believe that every pastor and church should determine what they consider to be appropriate and respectful dress for the worship service and then encourage that by example. By doing this, they will reverse the terrible slide into a sloppy, careless, and casual approach to God that is becoming disgraceful and distracting to the true worship of God. As a Reformed Baptist minister, I have always maintained a standard of wearing a suit and tie or a sport coat and tie for the official services of our church. I have required all those who preach in our pulpit to do the same. My personal reasons for this include the desire to be respectful to the office of a minister, to show to those who attend our services that we take worship seriously, and to demonstrate that we believe that how we approach God in worship truly matters. I have always believed that ministers who dress sloppy, casual, or who walk around in public unkempt, dirty or smelly are a terrible testimony to the world of our great Lord and His gospel. If God's servants do not dress professionally while discharging their duties, they will never garner the respect from the community in which they serve. If we do not take our ministries seriously, why should anyone else take them seriously? I am challenging all pastors and churches to reconsider how they approach God in the worship service. It is my conviction that casual dress by pastors and ministers, along with the sloppy dress in the church service, is not helping us in our worship of the living God. Casual dress by pastors and people in the worship service is sadly a sign of the times. The church has been influenced by a casual and careless culture rather than influencing the culture itself.

1

What Do The Scriptures Have To Say About Casual Dress In Worship?

"...there is nothing more perilous to our salvation than a preposterous and perverse worship of God."
                                                    John Calvin

Let me say up front that I have many good friends and brothers in Christ who often, if not nearly always, dress down and are casual in their ministry. I do not doubt the love they have for the Lord or the sincere desire they display for glorifying God and preaching the gospel. Many of these dear brothers and friends are very sincere in their walk with God. But this does not remove the concern that I have, that how they dress is sending a wrong message to those they minister to and to the watching world at large. This practice of dressing down and being casual is new in the church. It has not always been this way. I believe the changes that we have made in the way many dress in the pulpit is not wise or beneficial to the cause of Christ. It is my sincere belief that these things, in the long run, do more harm than good. To those dear brothers and friends, I humbly ask you to listen to me and give some thought to what I am saying here and see if the Holy Spirit does not, in some measure, speak to your soul about these matters.

One of the things I often hear people say who are advocates of casual dress for worship is that this will help encourage those who have no interest in church to attend. It is claimed that one of the major hurdles keeping non-churched people from entering the house of God is the way Christians dress on Sunday. It is believed by those who advocate "casual dress" that encouraging people to dress down on the Lord's Day will be an incentive to drawing the non-churched into our services. This reasoning is fallacious. Have we forgotten that the world has a built-in antipathy to the God of the Bible because of man's fall into sin in the garden? Changing how we dress, how we worship, and adding lots of entertainment or worldly attractions to our services is not the answer to the problem of how we get non-Christians to attend our worship services. How is it that so many theologically trained ministers have forgotten what Jesus said to Nicodemus in John 3:3? Jesus said, *"You must be born again."* Apart from the new birth that changes the heart of a man born in sin, that man will never hunger and thirst for God, long for worship, or delight in spiritual things. Unspiritual people have no desire for these things because they are spiritually dead in trespasses and sins. I am convinced that all of our new styles of music, dress, and ways of doing church have only been successful in diminishing the effectiveness of the church and making it more worldly.

Dressing down and encouraging a casual approach to God has weakened our testimony and has helped to fill many of our churches with those who have never been born again. We have made the church like the world and have lost our ability to be salt and light to our culture. Let me ask those of you who are now worshipping in a church that has adopted a casual dress code for worship—how effective has it been? How is it working for you? How many non-churched people have you really drawn to your church? Other than the fact that many who adopt casual dress gloat about their new found freedom, what has it really accomplished? Mega churches for years have been turning worship services into giant entertainment events. And many of those who have been the greatest advocates of this new trend have now admitted that it has not worked. They have replaced preaching with programs and replaced prayer with publicity. All that has been accomplished by these new methods has been the diminishing of true spiritual worship and, if anything, it has filled our churches with those who come for the entertainment and not the worship of God.

I want you to stop and consider the question that I raised in the beginning of this discussion, *"Does casual dress in our worship services by both the ministry and the laity, enhance or distract from biblical worship?"* We must find the answer to this question from the Word of God itself. There are no verses in the Bible that simply state, *"Thou shalt not come to church dressed casually."* But there are many verses, when taken together and carefully examined, strongly suggest that how we dress when we come to church is of great importance. When we consider these biblical passages and conclude that they are teaching us that dress does matter in our approach to God, we are making an inference based on the evidence drawn from these verses. To reason by way of inference is not an invalid approach to theology. There are a number of doctrines that we hold that are based on inference, the doctrine of the Trinity being one of them. There is no verse in the Bible that uses the word "trinity," but we glean from many verses that the doctrine of the Holy Trinity is a biblical truth.

Let's look at some of the verses in the Bible that relate, either directly or indirectly, to this subject of how we should dress and act when in the presence of God.

Old Testament Verses

When we read the instructions that were given in the Old Testament on how to worship God, we see careful details have been outlined to guide the way Israel worshipped the Lord. Exodus 28:1-8 tells us,

> "Now take Aaron your brother, and his sons with him, from among the children of Israel, that he may minister to Me as priest, Aaron and Aaron's sons: Nadab, Abihu, Eleazar, and Ithamar. ²And **you shall make holy garments for Aaron your brother, for glory and for beauty**. ³So you shall speak to all who are gifted artisans, whom I have filled with the spirit of wisdom, that they may make Aaron's garments, to consecrate him, that he may minister to Me as priest. ⁴And these are the garments which they shall make: a breastplate, an ephod, a robe, a skillfully woven tunic, a turban, and a sash. So they shall make holy garments for Aaron your brother and his sons, that he may minister to Me as priest."

Holy garments were made for glory and beauty that gave honor and dignity to the priests of the Lord. The point being made is that worship is serious business. Nothing should be done carelessly, casually, or in a flippant and disrespectful manner. Should not the ministers of God's new covenant of sovereign grace honor their calling and their office by reverence and by dressing in a way that is fit for the occasion?

Leviticus 16:1-6 gives instructions on how Aaron, the High Priest, is to approach God in worship. Notice as we read this passage the mention of holy garments.

> *"Now the Lord spoke to Moses after the death of the two sons of Aaron, when they offered profane fire before the Lord, and died; ²and the Lord said to Moses: "Tell Aaron your brother not to come at just any time into the Holy Place inside the veil, before the mercy seat which is on the ark, lest he die; for I will appear in the cloud above the mercy seat. ³Thus Aaron shall come into the Holy Place: with the blood of a young bull as a sin offering, and of a ram as a burnt offering.* **⁴He shall put the holy linen tunic and the linen trousers on his body; he shall be girded with a linen sash, and with the linen turban he shall be attired. These are holy garments. Therefore he shall wash his body in water, and put them on.** *⁵And he shall take from the congregation of the children of Israel two kids of the goats as a sin offering, and one ram as a burnt offering. ⁶"Aaron shall offer the bull as a sin offering, which is for himself, and make atonement for himself and for his house."*

The priests of the Old Testament were given careful instructions on when to come into God's presence and also how to dress when they approached Jehovah in temple worship. Their dress code gave them a standing of respect, honor, and dignity. We are not bound by the dress code given in the Old Testament. But it is wise to remember that each believer today is a priest unto the Lord. I Peter 2:9 reads, *"But you are a chosen generation, a royal priesthood, a holy nation, His own special people..."* As priests under the New Covenant, do you suppose that God would be less concerned than He was about His priests under the Old Covenant? I believe this principle still applies. When leading a worship service, we should dress in a way that does not in any way lesson our authority, detract from our holy calling as ambassadors for Christ, or identify us with those elements in our culture that are opposed to the God of heaven.

In Zechariah 3:3-5 we read,

> "Now Joshua was clothed with filthy garments, and was standing before the Angel. ⁴Then He answered and spoke to those who stood before Him, saying, "Take away the filthy garments from him." And to him He said, "See, I have removed your iniquity from you, and I will clothe you with rich robes." ⁵And I said, "Let them put a clean turban on his head." So they put a clean turban on his head, and they put the clothes on him. And the Angel of the Lord stood by."

Commenting on this passage a Presbyterian minister said,

> "there is a theological and ecclesiological motive behind many who preach in casual clothing such as jeans and possibly even T-shirts, and that this motive has the effect of de-solemnizing worship. This is because their motive is to make visitors and members feel more comfortable and less intimidated. But the hallmark of solemnity and reverence is not, or at least should not, be comfort. The stated motive of these PCA ministers is usually to teach the congregation that God accepts them just as they are and presumably that they can come before Him just as they are. But passages like Zechariah 3:3-5 show that external garments, particularly of the priest/pastor, speak to the congregation, and indicate something of the majesty of God and His worthiness."[1]

If the Old Testament teaches us anything about worship, it teaches us that how we come before the Lord is extremely important. We are not obligated to wear those same garments today under the New Covenant that the Old Testament priests wore. But is there not some wise instruction and practical lessons that we might glean from these Old Covenant passages? I think there is. Those who dismiss these verses so quickly do so unwisely. The priests in the Old Testament were forbidden to have a casual approach to God in worship both by attitude and by their dress. I think there is a principle that we can and should learn from this. These Old Testament passages teach us that sloppy and careless dress when coming into the presence of God for corporate worship where His glory, honor, and majesty are revealed is not appropriate for such exalted and heavenly worship.

Genesis 35:1-3 sheds some light on how we approach God in worship. The text reads:

> *"Then God said to Jacob, "Arise, go up to Bethel and dwell there; and make an altar there to God, who appeared to you when you fled from the face of Esau your brother." ²And Jacob said to his household and to all who were with him, "Put away the foreign gods that are among you, **purify yourselves, and change your garments**. ³Then let us arise and go up to Bethel; and I will make an altar there to God, who answered me in the day of my distress and has been with me in the way which I have gone."*

Here we see that God told Jacob that preparation is to be taken both in cleanliness and dress when one approaches Him in worship.

In the Mosaic law there were certain standards for the priests and for the people in how they dressed and how they approached God in worship. In Exodus 28:1-43 we find some of these principles taught.

> "Now take Aaron your brother, and his sons with him, from among the children of Israel, that he may minister to Me as priest, Aaron and Aaron's sons: Nadab, Abihus, Eleazar, and Ithamar. ²And **you shall make holy garments for Aaron your brother, for glory and for beauty**. ³So you shall speak to all who are figured artisans, whom I have filled with the spirit of wisdom, that they may make Aaron's garments to consecrate him, that he may minister to Me as priest." [Exodus 28:1-3]

These garments were to be holy. In other words, the clothing that the priests wore during worship was set apart and dedicated to the worship of God. These garments distinguished the priests from the others at worship. In verse 36 we see the main principle in making these priestly garments was the "holiness" of God.

When Samuel the prophet was interviewing the sons of Jesse to find the Lord's anointed, he made the mistake of judging the brothers by sight and not by spiritual qualifications. In I Samuel 16:7 we are told,

> "But the Lord said to Samuel, 'Do not look at his appearance or at the height of his stature, because I have refused him. For the Lord does not see as man sees; for man looks at the outward appearance, but the Lord looks at the heart.'"

Some people conclude from this verse that outward dress in worship is not that important. Man looks on the outward appearance, but God looks at our heart. But it is also true that the outward man often reflects what going on in his inner man or in his heart. The Scripture says, *"As a man thinks in his heart so is he."* Proverbs 21:10. How a man dresses reveals much about his inner soul. It is a terrible mistake to draw the conclusion from this verse in I Samuel that how we dress in the corporate worship of God does not matter. The world can be fooled by the outer man. This does not mean that the outer man is incon-sequential. Both what we are inwardly and how we behave and dress outwardly must be consistent with holiness. Are there any types of clothing that would be inappropriate to wear to a worship service? Of course there are. Therefore, those who are pure in heart, filled with the Holy Spirit, walking in reverence and in the fear of God will reflect that inner attitude by outward dress and demeanor.

Another Scripture to consider is Genesis 41:14. When Joseph was called upon to stand before Pharaoh the Scripture says, **"he shaved, changed his clothing, and came to Pharaoh"** When we come before the King of the universe to worship Him should we not show as much consideration for our Holy God that Joseph did for the king of Egypt? Jesus is the King of Kings and the Lord of Lords. Our approach to Him should always be filled with reverence and fear and trembling. When people dress casual, they often act casual. Being casual in the presence of God is not something that we should aim for. In every case in the Bible when people found themselves in the presence of God they were anything but relaxed and casual. Stunned, awed, filled with wonder, joy, praise, driven to their knees, overwhelmed, and made speechless are more accurate ways of describing people in the presence of God.

During the Old Covenant, the children of Israel did not casually approach Jehovah God in worship. They were not invited to "come as you are" to the tabernacle or temple to worship. God's people had to undergo purification rituals and bathe in pools before they could enter the temple. Nowhere in the Old or New Testaments were people ever encouraged to approach God in a casual manner.

In the Psalms, King David tells us that we must come before God with clean hands and pure hearts.

> *"Who may ascend into the hill of the Lord? Or who may stand in His holy place? ⁴He who has clean hands and a pure heart, Who has not lifted up his soul to an idol, Nor sworn deceitfully."* [Psalm 24:3-4.]

What David reminds us here is that there are serious things to consider when we approach God in worship. When we prepare for worship by cleansing our hearts and applying the blood and righteousness of Christ to our souls, and while preparing our hearts for worship by holy communion with God, are we aided in our worship of God by being casual and relaxed?

When we gather in the presence of God, we are to come with great humility, reverence, and with the fear of the Lord. Solomon, the son of David, tells us in Proverbs that, *"The fear of the Lord is the beginning of wisdom."* Proverbs 9:10. I suggest to you that this generation that has become so casual, carnal, and compromised with the world has lost much of the biblical concept of the fear of God. History teaches us that when the fear of God departs from any period in church history, the result is an increasing spirit of levity, shallowness, and irreverence. Most pastors who dress casual in their worship service will argue that they do fear the Lord. Only God knows their hearts. But I know this, by many years of experience, that the men I have met over the years who were known for their deep love of Christ and who were characterized by the fear of the Lord had a much higher view of the pulpit ministry than I have seen in many of these contemporary preachers who dress so casually when they preach.

Finally, we see in the Old Testament that some types of clothing are not only immodest and sensual, but have direct association to the dress of prostitutes and harlots. Proverbs 7:1-10 reads,

> *"My son, keep my words, And treasure my commands within you. ²Keep my commands and live, And my law as the apple of your eye. ³Bind them on your fingers; Write them on the tablet of your heart. ⁴Say to wisdom, "You are my sister," And call understanding your nearest kin, ⁵That they may keep you from the immoral woman, From the seductress who flatters with her words. ⁶For at the window of my house I looked through my lattice, ⁷And saw among the simple, I perceived among the youths, A young man devoid of understanding, ⁸Passing along the street near her corner; And he took the path to her house ⁹In the twilight, in the evening, In the black and dark night. ¹⁰And there a woman met him, With the attire of a harlot, and a crafty heart."*

Solomon warns young men to beware of those who dress with the *"attire of a harlot."* This text in Proverbs suggests that some styles of clothing identifies us with certain ungodly elements of society. Christians concerned about their testimony will be extremely cautious of dressing in a way that would identify them with those who are the enemies of God.

Over and over again we see that the Old Testament Scriptures teach us that how we dress in worship is of utmost importance.

New Testament Scriptures

When we discuss the way we should dress in the house of the Lord, James 2:1-4 will invariably be brought to our attention.

> *"My brethren, do not hold the faith of our Lord Jesus Christ, the Lord of glory, with partiality. ²For if there should come into your assembly a man with gold rings, in fine apparel, and there should also come in a poor man in filthy clothes, ³and you pay attention to the one wearing the fine clothes and say to him, "You sit here in a good place," and say to the poor man, "You stand there," or, "Sit here at my footstool," ⁴have you not shown partiality among yourselves, and become judges with evil thoughts?"*

Of course, I agree with these verses. In all the years of my ministry I have never seen any poor person come to our services that were treated rudely, unkindly, or turned away from our church. I have not heard of this kind of behavior in other churches, either. This text in James does not encourage ministers to dress down in the pulpit. To use this verse to justify casual dress in worship is missing the point of what James is saying. James is giving us a lesson on being fair and impartial with all people. James just uses a rich man and a poor man to make the point of sinful partiality among God's people in the church.

Paul the apostle writes in I Timothy 2:9, *"in like manner also, that the women adorn themselves in modest apparel, with propriety and moderation, not with braided hair or gold or pearls or costly clothing,"* Here the apostle is telling us that when women come to church they should be mindful of modesty. Some types of clothing worn by women are just not appropriate for godly women to wear. This is not to suggest that casual dress is immodest, although it often is! Many times casual dress is simply less dress. No pastor wants to enforce legalistic dress codes on the church that are not found in the Bible. But faithful ministers must insist on the standards and principles taught by Jesus and His apostles. This verse is one of them. No one should ever say that the Pastor or leaders of the church have nothing to say about how we dress or how we come dressed to the worship service. Immodesty is prohibited by the Word of God.

In the book of Acts we read,

> "There was a certain man in Caesarea called Cornelius, a centurion of what was called the Italian Regiment, ²a devout man and one who feared God with all his household, who gave alms generously to the people, and prayed to God always. ³About the ninth hour of the day he saw clearly in a vision an angel of God coming in and saying to him, "Cornelius!" ⁴And when he observed him, he was afraid, and said, "What is it, lord?" So he said to him, "Your prayers and your alms have come up for a memorial before God. ⁵Now send men to Joppa, and send for Simon whose surname is Peter. ⁶ He is lodging with Simon, a tanner, whose house is by the sea. He will tell you what you must do." ⁷And when the angel who spoke to him had departed, Cornelius called two of his household servants and a devout soldier from among those who waited on him continually. ⁸So when he had explained all these things to them, he sent them to Joppa. ⁹The next day, as they went on their journey and drew near the city, Peter went up on the housetop to pray, about the sixth hour. ¹⁰Then he became very hungry and wanted to eat; but while they made ready, he fell into a trance ¹¹and saw heaven opened

and an object like a great sheet bound at the four corners, descending to him and let down to the earth. 12In it were all kinds of four-footed animals of the earth, wild beasts, creeping things, and birds of the air. 13And a voice came to him, "Rise, Peter; kill and eat." 14But Peter said, "Not so, Lord! For I have never eaten anything common or unclean." 15And a voice spoke to him again the second time, "What God has cleansed you must not call common." [Acts 10:1-15]

This is the story of how God revealed to Peter that Gentiles were no longer to be considered unclean. This lesson was absolutely essential for the new church in its infancy to be able to distinguish between things that were holy (set apart) and things that were profane, (common or ungodly). I use the principle here to point out that many people in the church today, and even pastors and ministers, lack the ability to distinguish between things that are holy or profane. I have seen people wear things to church that were not only immodest but were extremely sensual and fleshly.

Again, we see that certain styles and modes of dress are certainly inappropriate for those who are the children of God. In I Thessalonians 5:22 the apostle Paul exhorts his readers, *"Abstain from all appearance of evil."* The Apostle's exhortation supports the verse in Proverbs 7 that godly women are to avoid the appearance of wearing the clothing that would be typical of those who are prostitutes. This verse in I Thessalonians 5 can apply to any kind of clothing that would identify us in any way that was less than godly or respectable. We should avoid dressing like those who are the most ungodly in our society. When you see young people coming to church dressed like rock stars, drug pushers, pimps, gangsters or hoodlums, we should remember I Thessalonians 5:22, *"Abstain from all appearance of evil."*

The point of these verses is not just to remind ourselves of immodest dress and attire but also to teach us that how we dress does send a message to others. The way we dress in the house of God is of great importance. The way God's people dress when they come to church sends a message to all who attend the service. What we wear out in public sends a message to others as well.

The apostle Paul teaches us that whatever we do in the church should be done *"...decently and in order."* I Corinthians 14:40. This implies that there can be many things done in dress and practice that are not decent and in order. The pastor and leaders of a church must think carefully about what they are doing when they make a decision to reject centuries of tradition and dress casually as if this is an appropriate thing to do.

We are not under certain aspects of the Law of Moses today. There were civil and ceremonial laws that no longer apply to the New Covenant church. But we must not forget what the apostle Paul tells us in Romans 15:4 and I Corinthians 10:11. *"For whatever things were written before were written for our learning, that we through the patience and comfort of the Scriptures might have hope,"* Romans 15:4. In I Corinthians 10:11 we read, *"Now all these things happened to them as examples, and they were written for our admonition, upon whom the ends of the ages have come."* The apostle Paul is teaching us that the Old Testament still has application for us today and the many principles taught there were for our instruction. With this in mind, are we making a massive error when we discard the principles that we derive from the teachings of the Old Testament on worship? In the Old Testament the priests were given special garments that set them apart for worship. These garments were for their honor and their dignity as the servants of the Most High God. Do these principles not apply to us today? Is Sunday worship, which is throne-room worship, any less important today than was temple worship in the Old Testament? I declare to you that there is nothing more important than worship on the Lord's Day. We are told by the apostle Paul that we are not to forsake the assembling of ourselves together as some apparently did. To come into the presence of God flippantly and casually is one of the greatest insults one could give to the King of Heaven.

Believers are indeed a royal priesthood. They are the true tabernacle of God. With this in mind, do you really think that God is not concerned in this new covenant period with how His ministers dress or how His people draw near to Him? Dress is symbolic. How we dress when we gather for public and corporate worship sends a message to all who see us. In other faiths such as Islam and in many of the Eastern religions, Imams and Priests still dress with religious garments that convey symbolic messages to those who worship with them. Only in Christendom do we see Ministers, Priests, and Pastors dumbing down the worship and dressing down to try to be more relatable. The question we must ask is "How wise is this?"

The casual manner in which many come to church today and in which so many ministers today dress when they lead a worship service is hindering rather than helping the cause of Christ. It may sound pious or spiritual to claim we are free to come before the Lord casually, but as we have seen from Scripture and as we will see from tradition and common sense, it would be wise for God's servants to rethink what they are doing and what they are communicating by their casual dress when they approach God in worship. Every Christian understands that there are moments when we are suddenly called upon to rush into the presence of God to intercede for others or for ourselves. We may, at times, be thrust into emergency situations where we are compelled to pray and seek God's face without any time to prepare ourselves for these moments. No one denies that this often happens to us as believers. This is not an argument to suggest that it does not matter how we dress or how we prepare ourselves for worship. There will be times when we have no time to think about dress when we come before the Lord. But when we come to the Lord's Day, there is no rush or reason why we cannot pause and prepare our hearts carefully and thoroughly. Considering our dress is one of the things we do when we have important and serious events to attend. What can be more important than coming into the presence of God? I see Lord's Day worship as the high point of our week. Lord's Day worship is more profound than any wedding or funeral. We should dress as though we believed this.

The apostle Paul in Romans chapter twelve said, *"Do not be conformed to this world but be ye transformed by the renewing of your mind, that ye may prove what is that good and perfect and acceptable will of 'God."* Romans 12:2. The word "conformed" means to be fashioned or made into the likeness of something. When Pastors and churches embrace casual dress for worship are they not conforming to the spirit of the age? This verse, like the others we have considered, does not directly speak to the issue of casual dress for worship, but the principle does apply.

When we search the Scriptures to see how men reacted when they drew near to God and when they found themselves in the presence of God, we see nothing that would indicate a casual or careless approach to the Most High God. Moses (Exodus 3) trembles on the holy mountain and is told to remove his sandals. Isaiah (Isaiah 6) trembles and is overwhelmed by the vision of God in the temple. Job, (Job 40) when he encounters the Lord after all of his complaining and whining, falls prostate before God with silent lips. Peter, when he senses he is in the presence of God cries out to the Lord Jesus, *"Depart from me for I am a sinful man."* And Saul (Acts 9) on the road to Damascus falls to the ground in a state of shock at the presence of the risen Christ.

Finally, in the book of Revelation when John is on the Isle of Patmos and meets the risen Christ (Revelation 1), falls down as though he were a dead man. A careful study of throne-room worship in the book of Revelation reveals not only the saints in glory were full of reverence but even the angels are marked by a holy awe and wonder. There is no hint of casual worship in heaven.

We must ask ourselves several questions and answer them honestly. Is there not a principle of a "proper decorum" that is becoming to the worship of the Most High God of Heaven? Do we not send, perhaps, the wrong message to those who sit under our ministries and to the world when we dress down and come to worship as if we were going to a football game, going fishing, or going out to clean the garage? Have the pastors and people who have promoted casual dress in worship ever stopped to consider whether or not the dignity and sanctity of true worship is being undermined by their casual dress? Some pastors even make the boast that they are "cool." How does this fit with being holy and reverent? Some pastors dress like they are attending a college fraternity. This may be cool, sharp, and contemporary, but it is not appropriate for the servant of the Lord, who stands in the holy pulpit as an ambassador of the Most High God. What we wear in the pulpit and to church communicates a great deal to those who attend our services whether we like it or not. This comment says it all:

> *"Clothes say something about what we think, what we value. They also influence how we behave and feel. That our culture has become so casual about everything says something about us. I cannot exactly articulate it but it seems to say, "nothing is really all that important." But that is not true. Going to God's house IS important. Being ministered to by the King of Kings and Lord of Lords is astounding. Casual attire in these circumstances is simply inappropriate if we really think about what we are doing, where we are going and who it is we will meet."[2]*

I have sought to show from both the Old and New Testament Scriptures that there is a proper way to come to the Lord's house to worship. We learn many lessons from the instructions that the Lord gave the priests of the Old Testament. I know that there will be those who will reject what I am saying, and they will give any number of reasons why dressing casually for worship by both the preachers and the members of the church makes sense. Here is a summary of the arguments that are often used to justify casual dress by ministers in our worship services:

1. The Bible tells us we are to be all things to all men. I Corinthians 9:22-23.
2. We are not under that law so the Old Testament Mosaic law does not apply to us anymore.
3. We can reach more people this way (the end justifies the means).
4. When people are dressed casual, they will find that worship is much more enjoyable.

5. Those who advocate dress codes of any kind are legalistic and are acting like Pharisees.
6. We are to live by the New Testament, and the New Testament is silent on the subject of how ministers should dress for worship or how people should dress for worship.
7. People who are unchurched (unsaved) prefer casual dress if they are going to church for worship.

    The **first** argument states, the Bible tells us we are to *"become all things to all men, that I might by all means save some."* I Corinthian 9:22-23. Answer: Paul's comments in this verse have been used by many through the centuries to justify becoming like the world in order to win the world. We can dress any way we want and use any music we want if doing this enables us to win more men to Christ. This has meant that nearly every ungodly and worldly activity or attraction has been used by the church to draw the unchurched to their services. Everyone agrees that this verse must be restricted by God's law. This text has to do with issues that are not essential. Worship is massively essential. Did this teaching by the apostle Paul really give the church license to do what ever they wanted so that they could win more people to Christ? This is not what the apostle Paul meant. He did not mean that the pastor should become a drunkard to win alcoholics to Christ, or that a Christian mother should become a prostitute to win prostitutes to Christ, and so on. Paul the apostle was passionate about winning people to Christ, but he never advocated sinning as a method of doing so. Paul would never compromise on the Word of God, or tolerate sin in his life and justify it, if it gave him an opportunity to win others to the Lord. The apostle Paul was no slick advertiser, con-artist, or marketing guru who twisted the Bible every which way so as to accommodate his life style to the ways of sinful men. The question then remains, "What did Paul mean when he wrote these words?" To become all things to all men does not in any way suggest that we accommodate to any and all ungodly practices or compromise on biblical law and principle. This applies only to matters of indifference. And if we make accommodations to other cultures on matters of indifference, we must never draw the conclusions that those accommodations are morally binding on our consciences.

The **second** argument states, "We are not under the law so the Old Testament does not apply to us any more." Answer: I Corinthians 9:22 tells us that we are under the law of Christ. That we are not under the law does not mean we can ignore the law or the Old Testament for that matter. Paul tells us the law is holy, just and good, and that it must be used correctly. Paul quotes a number of the Ten Commandments in Romans chapter 13 verse 8-10, so Paul did not consider that the moral aspects of God's law has no impact on us. Everything in the Old Testament applies to the New Covenant believer. The question is, "How does it apply?" The Old Testament law was our school master to lead us to Christ. Galatians 3:24. Although we are no longer under the law's heavy weight of bondage, the law still has a purpose in our lives:

1. The law is our school master to convict us of sin and to lead us to the Savior.
2. The law teaches us what sin is.
3. The law is our spiritual sentinel and stands guard over us and protects us.
4. The law reveals the mind and the will of God to us.
5. The law shows us how to live in this fallen world.

By rejecting the law of God outright, we fall into antinomianism which is a dangerous heresy. The church is facing an epidemic of this anti-law attitude within the church in our generation. We can summarize and say that the three uses of the law are:

1. To be a mirror to show us our sin.
2. To serve as a restraint to sin.
3. To reveal God's will and law to us.

We are not under the law as a means of justification. But the law still has these three very important functions.

Paul never intended to leave the New Testament Church under the impression that the believer was no longer obliged to the law in any way. As we have seen in this chapter Paul tells us that what we read in the Old Testament was for our instruction and serves as types and examples for us. There are many issues that are addressed in the Old Testament law that are not mentioned in the New Testament. The apostle Paul tells us in Romans 15:4 and I Corinthians 10:11: *"For whatever things were written before were written for our learning, that we through the patience and comfort of the Scriptures might have hope."* Romans 15:4. And in I Corinthians 10:11 we read, *"Now all these things happened to them as examples, and they were written for our admonition, upon whom the ends of the ages have come."* Clearly, the apostle Paul is telling us that the Old Testament law and all the teaching of its types, shadows, symbols and stories were given for our edification and instruction. If we reject outright the entire law, then we are left in the dark on many moral issues and concerns. It is certainly valid to draw from the Old Testament many principles and lessons that we can apply to our Christian life.

The **third** argument states, "We can reach more people this way (the end justifies the means)." Answer: This is a way of saying that by dressing down in the pulpit, ministers will be less offensive and will draw more people to the church. We do not worship in ways to please the unbeliever; we worship in ways to please God. The problem with such a pragmatic approach is that it fails to remember the fall of man. Man is unregenerate and has a natural antipathy towards spiritual things. Man, if left to himself, will always reject the gospel unless he is born again and given the gift of faith and repentance. When it comes to the Word of God, the end never justifies the means. We are obligated to obey the Word of God and all of God's holy laws and principles.

The **fourth** argument states, "When people are dressed casually, they will find that worship is much more enjoyable." Answer: This is an immature viewpoint that does not take into account the significance and seriousness of the worship event. There are those who do not dress casually and find worship to be very joyful, satisfying and significant. So this is faulty reasoning. This is not a debate over how much we enjoy worship. It is a debate over the significance of this event. Is there spiritual joy in seeing the awesome significance of throne-room worship? Absolutely! The very nature of arguments like these is that those who advocate them are seeking to accommodate the world, and by doing so are compromising with the world. To dress sloppy, careless, casual, or in any way that identifies one with certain aspects of the fallen culture around them is degrading to the high calling that a minister has from the Lord. Is it not interesting that in the Old Testament we never see the High Priest making such accommodations with the world unless he is involved in wholesale apostasy. The truth must be told that biblical worship is never agreeable to the old nature of fallen man until he is crushed by the power of the convictions of the Holy spirit and is humbled in the dust before the cross of Christ. Until a sinner is humbled, broken, convicted, and spiritually brought low at the foot of the cross, he will never find true worship enjoyable. Casual dress, clever marketing strategies, carnal innovations, and compromising ministers will not fill the church with true worshippers. When we make the church like the world, we must not be surprised if the world comes pouring in but for all the wrong reasons. Those churches that adopt new but worldly strategies will give an account some day before the Lord for filling His kingdom with tares.

The **fifth** argument states, "Those who advocate dress codes of any kind are legalistic and are acting like Pharisees." Answer: Everyone has a dress code. No one would allow people to come to church nude or in a bathing suit. The issue is which dress code is to be accepted. No matter which dress code someone enforced, somebody could say it was too strict or legalistic. To call those who are committed to obeying the Word of God "Pharisees or legalists" is a serious charge. Pharisees were guilty of teaching as the doctrines of God the ideas of man. When we use the Scriptures to determine how we worship, we hardly pass as Pharisees. The clear teachings of God's Word in both the Old and New Testaments is the basis for all that we believe and practice.

The **sixth** argument states, "We are to live by the New Testament and the New Testament is silent on the subject of how ministers and people should dress for worship." Answer: In heaven everyone is dressed in white robes. Jesus said everything will be done on earth as it is in heaven. Why were the Roman soldiers gambling for the robe of Christ? Is it possible that the Lord's robe may have been either an expensive or beautiful priestly robe? Furthermore, the New Testament Scriptures are not completely silent on the subject of how we dress. There are verses in both the Old and New Testaments that teach either directly or by way of inference how we should dress when we approach God in worship. When we add up the verses, principles, holy examples, and exhortations from both the Old and New Testaments, we have a very clear idea of what God expects from those who serve Him in the ministry. Where is the burden of proof on this matter? Does the Bible not seem to indicate that there is a special way that God's servants should dress when proclaiming His Word in worship? I believe it does.

The **seventh** argument states, "People who are unchurched (unsaved) prefer casual dress if they are going to church for worship." Answer: This is a ridiculous argument. Never before in the history of the church have Christian leaders gone to the world to take a poll to see what they want for worship. It's only been in recent years that the church has polled those who know the least about true biblical worship to help them determine how they should conduct their services and worship God. Furthermore, we aren't surprised that those who are unchurched or who don't know the Lord would want something that would please their flesh. Many unchurched people might prefer we serve beer and pizza on Sundays and scrap the preaching altogether and replace it with something more entertaining. The servant of God must listen to God's Word and not put any confidence in the preferences of fallen men.

People have joked about Dr. Martyn Lloyd-Jones sitting on a beach wearing a suit and tie. I'm not suggesting that we all follow his example and wear a suit and tie at the beach, but I am asking you to ask yourself why he would do that? It was not because he only had suits and ties to wear. And I will suggest that it's unfair to say that this was just some odd quirk about his personality. I believe the reason he dressed that way, even in times of relaxation or on holiday, is because he held such a high view of the ministry. He saw himself as a servant of the Most High God. He took his calling to the office as a Pastor and Preacher of the gospel very seriously. Dr. Lloyd-Jones knew that he was a representative of the High King of heaven. He was an ambassador for God. When people were in his presence, they saw a man who was holy, devout, serious, and reverent. Maybe we are a little too hard on Dr. Lloyd-Jones when we smirk at his pictures on the beach wearing a suit and tie. Many of today's preachers could stand to have a little of the dignity, respect, and reverence of the good doctor.

    I knew another man who nearly always wore either a coat and tie or a suit and tie. My father-in-law, Dr. Del Fehsenfeld, was an evangelist from the deep South. He dressed in such a way that always displayed a high view of his calling as a minister and a preacher of the gospel. He saw himself as always on duty and on call. He took every opportunity to witness or testify to the gospel of the Lord Jesus Christ. Dressing that way did not in any way hurt his image or cause people to disrespect him. Quite the contrary. He was deeply respected because of the dignity in the way he dressed. He dressed as if he took his calling seriously. Too many ministers today give the impression they are playing at their calling. Dr. Lloyd-Jones and my father-in-law set an example and were men who respected the office as a minister of God and of the New Covenant. By their attitude and dress they demonstrated the fact that they were always on call, ready to preach, teach, witness or minister, and people saw them that way. Some how

I feel that many ministers today could use a little of their dignity, devotion, and reverence.

In the next chapter, we will see that the history of the church with its rich traditions and holy examples should instruct us on this subject of casual worship. Ours is a generation that is removing the ancient landmarks. This generation is creating new and unbiblical methods of worship. Today, many ministers approach God with a casual swagger and arrogance that is unbecoming those who are His holy ones called and set aside as the elect of God to worship Him in the beauty of holiness.

Verses Referenced In This Chapter

Old Testament
Genesis 35:1-3
Genesis 41:14
Exodus 3
Exodus 28:1-43
Exodus 28:1-3
Leviticus 16:1-6
I Samuel 16:7
Job 40
Psalms 24:3-4
Proverbs 7:1-10
Proverbs 9:10
Isaiah 6

New Testament
John 3:3
Acts 9
Acts 10:1-15
Romans 12:2
Romans 15:4
I Corinthians 10:11
I Corinthians 14:40
Galatians 3:24
I Thessalonians 5:22
I Timothy 2:9
James 2:1-4
I Peter 1:19
I Peter 2:9
Revelation 1

2

What Does Tradition Have To Say About Casual Dress In Worship?

"Worship is no longer worship when it reflects the culture around us more than the Christ within us."

A. W. Tozer

I believe the reason for much of the theological "drift" and "compromise" found in today's church is due to the fact, among other things, that the church has forsaken the "holy traditions" that have been passed down through the ages. The word *"tradition"* means, "the delivery of opinion, doctrines, practices, rites, and customs from generation to generation by oral communication."[1] Traditions are the established, or customary patterns of thought, behavior and practices in a religious or secular community. The word "tradition" is from the Latin word "traditio" and means, "action of handing over." The Greek word for traditions is "paradosis" and means handing over or passing down. When someone learns something from someone else, a tradition has taken place. Traditions deliver to one generation from another generation things that are priceless. These traditions include language, cultural customs, religious practices, holidays, sports, and standards of public and private behavior.

Those who reject the role of traditions in the church often cite the statements of Jesus on this subject. Jesus warned against the false traditions of men. In Matthew 15: 2-10 Jesus said:

> *"Why do Your disciples transgress the **tradition** of the elders? For they do not wash their hands when they eat bread."* ³*He answered and said to them, "Why do you also transgress the commandment of God because of your tradition? ⁴For God commanded, saying, 'Honor your father and your mother'; and, 'He who curses father or mother, let him be put to death.' ⁵But you say, 'Whoever says to his father or mother, "Whatever profit you might have received from me is a gift to God"–* ⁶*then he need not honor his father or mother.' Thus you have made the commandment of God of no effect **by your tradition**.* ⁷*Hypocrites! Well did Isaiah prophesy about you, saying:* ⁸*'These people draw near to Me with their mouth, And honor Me with their lips, But their heart is far from Me.* ⁹*And in vain they worship Me, Teaching as doctrines the commandments of men.'"*

Jesus took issue with the perversion of God's Word by man-made traditions. He was not against those holy traditions handed down (paradosis) through the ages from the ancient church. The Apostle Paul spoke of good traditions in I Corinthians 11:2 and in II Thessalonians 2:15, 3:6:

> *"Now I praise you, brethren, that you remember me in all things and **keep the traditions** just as I delivered them to you."* [I Corinthians 11:2]

*"Therefore, brethren, stand fast and **hold the traditions** which you were taught, whether by word or our epistle."* [II Thessalonians 2:15]

*"But we command you, brethren, in the name of our Lord Jesus Christ, that you withdraw from every brother who walks disorderly and not according to **the tradition** which he received from us."* [II Thessalonians 3:6]

Dr. R. C. Sproul had this to say about traditions:

"As Protestants, we sometimes see the word tradition and immediately throw up our guard because of the way we have seen traditions used to deny the Word of God and bind consciences with the straitjacket of legalism. Yet, it is important to realize that tradition in itself can be a neutral or even a good thing. The tradition that some churches have of meeting at 11 a.m. for worship on the Lord's Day is neither good nor bad in itself. It usually reflects, in fact, the prudential judgment of the church's leadership. Expressions of tradition such as the Apostles' Creed or the Westminster Confession of Faith are good things, for these statements of faith can help us better understand the Word of God. All of us bring some tradition to our reading of Scripture, our hearing of the preached Word of God, and so forth." [2]

Dr. Sproul speaks of "prudential judgment of the church's leadership." If we are going to reject the "traditions" of how ministers should dress in the pulpit, we must first demonstrate that the wisdom and prudential judgment of the leaders of the church had it all wrong in the first place.

There are rich and wonderful traditions that have been handed down to us through the ages that we in our western civilization cherish and follow. We would be greatly impoverished if we forsake these traditions. But this is exactly what we are seeing today. Here are some examples of the traditions that have been handed down to us.

- We worship in traditional church buildings.
- We have ministers who wear white shirts, ties, and suits as they preach.
- We have a traditional midweek prayer service.
- We have a traditional Sunday Evening service in many churches.
- We received by tradition how we interpret the Word—historical/grammatical interpretation.
- We preach from a traditional pulpit.
- We received by tradition how the architecture of church buildings should look like.
- We have traditional steeples on many of our churches.
- We see many churches using traditional chimes or having a church bell.
- We see many ministers in different branches of Christendom wearing traditional clerical robes.
- We have a traditional turkey and Thanksgiving dinner.
- We have a traditional Christmas dinner.
- We put up traditional Christmas lights and decorations.
- We attend traditional Christmas Eve services.
- We have traditional Palm Sunday and Good Friday services before Easter.
- We see brides wearing traditional wedding dresses and veils.
- We repeat traditional vows at our weddings.
- We exchange traditional rings at our wedding ceremony.

- We see ministers wearing traditional suits for weddings and funerals.
- We see grooms wearing traditional tuxedoes at weddings.
- We sing traditional hymns for various Christian holidays.
- We celebrate many traditional holidays such as the Fourth of July and other special days.
- We see many families celebrating yearly family traditions.
- We say traditional prayers before our services.
- We see our soldiers following centuries long traditions and customs for the military.
- We see our presidents wearing a traditional suit at their inauguration and swearing in ceremony.
- We teach our children to follow the tradition of saying "please" and "thank you" and standing up when a woman enters the room.
- We teach our young men by tradition to be a gentleman and open the doors for ladies.
- We have certain traditions in nearly all of our institutions that we follow and observe.
- We practice the tradition of giving gifts at Christmas and on birthdays.
- We are asked by attorneys to wear a traditional suit at court cases.
- We have traditional songs for birthdays and other occasions.
- We give a traditional retirement party to those who retire.
- We send out by tradition cards for various occasions and holidays.

- We teach our children to say traditional prayers at bedtime.
- We read bedtime stories to our children by tradition.
- We practice family worship together by tradition.

Our culture is literally steeped in rich and historic traditions that we follow, cherish, and observe. But when it comes to how we worship—traditions are being thrown out the window! Many precious and rich traditions and values are being discarded and replaced by pop-culture, concepts of modernity, and worship is being watered-down to reflect the anti-Christian culture of neo-paganism. When families choose a church to attend, they often ignore the main spiritual criteria that should be used in selecting a church to worship in. Instead, many families often go to churches were they are entertained, where the messages are watered-down and are non-threatening. It is not uncommon for parents to relinquish their parental duties and allow the children to choose a place of worship. Children who are either unsaved or unspiritual should never be allowed to make one of the most important decisions in our life—namely, where we worship God.

Traditions are difficult to eradicate from a culture. Historically, the way traditions of various people groups are destroyed or diminished is by subjugation through invasion, mass migrations, and by cultural suicide when cultural traditions are forsaken for some new religion, philosophy or lifestyle. Today, in many parts of Europe and in some places in the United States, we no longer can sing Christmas carols, have nativity scenes, enjoy Christmas pageants, or display Christian symbols for fear of offending Muslims or atheists. Centuries of Christian traditions are being removed from our culture because of the fear of man. The onslaught against anything "traditional" or "western" is promoted by the philosophies of multi-culturalism, political correctness, anti-Christian values, anti-colonialism, anti-white, anti-male, or anti-judeo-Christian values. Today, "cultural diversity" is code for anti-Western and anti-Christian. I see casual dress in worship as a step in the direction of caving in to the forces that are seeking to unravel the rich and holy traditions of our faith.

Studies have shown that one way of destroying a civilization and a culture is to destroy or mock its traditions. Families, churches, and nations that have rich and vibrant traditions are more resilient to the pressures of modernity and are stronger because of them.

Traditions can be good things. We are greatly enriched by the treasure of traditions from the past. One church boldly put out on the marquee in front of the church this statement, **"We are untraditional; Check us out!"** Is this really a good thing to say? I think it is abominable. This is one of the major reasons the church today is adrift in a sea of relativity and confusion. A great theologian from the past, Richard Hooker (1554—1600) is said to have formulated the three legged stool approach for establishing authority in the church—Scripture, tradition, and reason. This does not mean we are abandoning the Reformed doctrine of Sola-Scriptura. It does mean, however, that if the church forgets to use reason and common sense, and fails to pay attention to holy traditions within the church that every Christian might become his or her own little Pope while all the wisdom from past Christian generations is forgotten. There are many wise and holy traditions that have been handed down to us from generation to generation. We would be greatly impoverished if we failed to recognize these valuable gifts from the past. All traditions must be evaluated by the Word of God. Any religious tradition that contradicts the

Scriptures must be rejected. But traditions such as the liturgical structure of worship, dress standards for ministers, church calendar, sacred holidays and things of this nature are a great blessing and benefit to the church. The Apostles Creed and the Nicene Creed are examples of holy traditions that have been passed down through the ages by the church. We would not allow anyone to join our church if they denied these two creeds. Tradition is important, but it is not the final or absolute authority. We test all traditions by the Word of God.

G. K. Chesterton describes tradition in this manner:

"Tradition means giving votes to the most obscure of all classes, our ancestors. It is the democracy of the dead. Tradition refuses to submit to that arrogant oligarchy (elite rulers) who merely happen to be walking around." [3]

Throughout church history there has been a long tradition of approaching God in worship with reverence and proper decorum. From the Eastern Orthodox church, Roman Catholic, Reformed, Independent, Baptists, Evangelical, and even Charismatic assemblies, the church has a tradition that sets an example before us on how to approach God in worship. It has not been until the later part of the twentieth century and into the first years of the twenty-first century that we are seeing a wide sweeping and calculated attempt to make worship in Christian churches informal, casual, and as a result, irreverent and common. The question we face today is this. *"Does casual dress in worship add to or detract from the true spiritual worship of God?"* It is my conviction that casual worship does detract from true spiritual worship. One pastor I know made these observations about casual worship:

"...we should never use the word "casual" as an adjective for worship. I know what is meant by it, or at least I think

> *I do. It seems that churches put this descriptor on their lighted marquee sign to announce to the world, "how you are dressed doesn't matter here." Or they are trying to convey to a culture that is obsessed with the comfortable that their service isn't traditional or firm or stiff or joyless. If this is the case, then I say, "Let the sign say that." I would have no problem with a church announcing on its sign, "Our 10:30 service at Crossroads Presbyterian is a "non-stiff" service." Just don't call it casual. Why? Because worship may be a lot of things, but it is never casual. Worship is an encounter with the living, true, holy, sovereign God of the universe."* [4]

This quote partially hits the mark in that it says, *"...worship may be a lot of things, but it is never casual."* I could not agree more. But his overall statement is self-contradictory in that it does not consider that how we dress may encourage a casual approach to God in worship. He agrees that "how you are dressed doesn't matter here." Really? Do they actually believe what they are saying? If people came naked, would that matter? If they came with t-shirts that had profanity on them, would that matter? Would they serve holy communion to those dressed like that? This pastor's quote raises the danger of casual worship but fails to address one of the root causes of casual worship which is the way some people dress. I would encourage the pastor who said this to not fear the religious establishment and make an application where it is needed to help prevent casual worship. This example shows a lack of understanding of the rich traditions of our Christian heritage.

Many pastors and people who defend the casual approach to God in worship disdain anything that is based on "tradition." Tradition is seen as some kind of mortal enemy to the Christian faith. If you even mention the word tradition you are mocked and sometimes viewed with pity.

One student of culture identified seven reasons why traditions are good for a culture and a country:

- *Tradition contributes a sense of comfort and belonging. It brings families together and enables people to reconnect with friends.*
- *Tradition reinforces values such as freedom, faith, integrity, a good education, personal responsibility, a strong work ethic, and the value of being selfless.*
- *Tradition provides a forum to showcase role models and celebrate the things that really matter in life.*
- *Tradition offers a chance to say "thank you" for the contribution that someone has made.*
- *Tradition enables us to showcase the principles of our Founding Fathers, celebrate diversity, and unite as a country.*
- *Tradition serves as an avenue for creating lasting memories for our families and friends.* [5]

The following comment reveals just how pervasive and successful this movement of casual dress in worship has become in removing the rich traditions we received from our spiritual fathers.

> "How odd it is that the current visible church is embracing diversity and multiculturalism uncritically, completely setting aside the wisdom of the early church fathers. There are congregations all around the country now that have multiple worship services, each in a different style to cater to the appetites of different target

groups. Of course what results is a conglomeration of separate congregations under one roof, each subcongregation demanding that its felt needs be met. It is group selfishness which does any thing but integrate the whole body of Christ." **6**

To summarize our thoughts, we may say that traditions are the rich treasures of the past that we pass down to those coming behind us that they too might be enriched by wisdom not their own. Traditions are like heir-looms; they are things of special value passed down from one generation to another. Tradition, then, is the handing down of information, beliefs, and cultural practices by repetition, word of mouth, and by example.

From all branches of the historic Christian church, we have received by tradition a clear example of ministerial dress and decorum when preaching the Word of God on the Lord's Day. This example, although differing from one branch to another, called for ministerial dress that reflected reverence, dignity, honor and respect for the calling of the New Covenant preacher.

Tradition, if it teaches us anything, teaches us the danger of causal worship.

3

What Does Common Sense Have To Say About Casual Dress In Worship?

"The worship of God must express a decorum and dignity appropriate to the meeting of God with his children."   Westminster Seminary, California

I find it hard to believe that so many ministers lack "common sense" when it comes to how to dress for worship. I can forgive the sheep for being easily influenced by a worldly culture, by being unable to discern what is holy and what is profane. But I find it more disturbing to understand why those called to the ministry have such poor judgment on these matters. Does not common sense teach us that we should dress and act in a way that fits or is appropriate for the occasion? How can anyone not see that the worship of God is vastly different from a picnic, ball game, fishing trip, or Saturday afternoon barbecue? When people trying to justify their casual dress in church and worship argue, "But we can worship God anywhere and in any clothing," it begs the issue. We all know that. The thief worshipped Jesus on the cross. The martyrs in England worshipped God as the flames engulfed their bodies. We can worship God in prison as did the Apostle Paul. But when we consider the example of the Scriptures, the rich traditions of our historic Christian faith, and common sense, we know that there are special occasions where our dress would be more appropriate if we were not dressed casual. The word, *"decorum"* means: "whatever is suitable or proper; propriety; fitness; propriety and good taste in behavior, speech, dress, etc.; an act or requirement of polite behavior."[1] The principle of acceptable decorum in the worship service of the King of Heaven would suggest that a worship service is more important to God than just trying to relate to an unregenerate world that has no interest in your worship in the first place. We gather in church services to worship God. We must not be surprised that the world does not desire to enter in to this holy hour before the Creator of the universe. Once people are truly regenerated (born again), they will have no problem of attending a worship service in the church of God. If you know your theology properly, you will know that worship is a matter of the heart, not of the surface emotion of making worship more appealing by being casual.

Does not common sense tell us that we dress in a certain way for weddings and funerals? Is it proper to officiate a funeral or wedding dressed in tennis shoes, shorts, a t-shirt or blue jeans? Think about it. One student of the cultural slide into casual worship stated the obvious,

> *"If you had the opportunity to meet the Queen of England, you wouldn't show up at Windsor Castle wearing jeans and a T-shirt,"* [2]

This judgment call is based on common sense. Why are there so few in the Lord's work today who display any signs of "common sense?" Where have the wise and saintly leaders gone who should be giving us wisdom and insight into the cultural confusion that has swept across this country like a tsunami? Another pastor says:

> "Different occasions call for different dress. You wear shorts, flip flops, and a tee shirt to lounge on the beach. It's a casual affair so casual attire is called for. If you had an audience with the President of the United States you would wear a coat and tie. Because of the gravity of the event, it would be flippant and disrespectful to wear your beach clothes." [3]

I have known young pastors who made a big deal about their freedom to worship casually and enjoyed flaunting that freedom only to put on a coat and tie for a funeral or wedding. Now, why did they dress up for the wedding or funeral? It was because of social customs and traditions. It was a sign of respect, and it was an occasion that called for something other than the causal. But to worship the God of the universe in clothing that would convey to us and others that worship is a very serious matter is thought to be legalistic. How tragic that this kind of thinking has permeated the vast majority of Christian churches. I think that we ministers will give an account to God on the day of judgement on how we led our worship services and what example we left those who sat under our ministries.

Common sense tells us that dressing for the occasion is beneficial for productivity and respect. It is difficult to understand how some ministers cannot see this. One minister made this comment:

> "If I am asked to wear business attire, I immediately think of an important event where business will be conducted. If I get to this event and the people I'm meeting have no agenda other than to sit around and chat, my first question is, "Why am I here, all dressed up?" When I put the suit and tie on for what I thought was business, I not only

dressed up for the occasion, my thoughts, attitude, and demeanor also became business-like. What I was wearing helped to define everything about me at that moment. Dressing up helps lift other parts of my life in an upward direction. Unfortunately, the opposite (dressing down) works the same way. Our dress can influence how we function. We should give proper consideration to what we look like, dressing appropriately for different occasions." 4

We dress in a casual way when doing yard work because we have a casual attitude towards such work. We wear casual clothes when participating in sporting events because these are indeed casual occasions. We wear casual clothes for casual events. Please explain to me why you would wear casual clothes to worship the God of the universe? Does not common sense tell us that this is just not right? If there is nothing sacred anymore, if there is nothing holy anymore, then where does this line of reasoning stop? Can pastors just do anything or wear anything in the act of worshipping God and then defend it by the cry, "I'm not under the law!" "I have freedom and liberty to do this?" "I am not a legalist!" Tell me where does your freedom to do whatever you think is right in the worship of Almighty God begin and end?

One student of our current situation in the Christian West made these insightful comments:

"Although our culture has trended in the casual direction, by no means has dressing up for important occasions gone out of style. People who have an important place in society still dress up to show respect for their vocation. Journalists, who report the day's news, dress professionally. So do lawyers, financial executives, and elected officials. Professional athletes are often required to

wear suits when traveling, and the hosts of late night TV all respect their place in the entertainment world by dressing for success. Stores need not worry; there is still sufficient demand for dress clothes by those in the world that recognize the importance of their place. There is one institution, however, where things have changed radically. Evangelical churches across America are led and attended by people who often look like they just rolled out of bed. Casual pants and an un-tucked shirt have become the uniform for today's preachers. What a sharp contrast to those who coach basketball teams, where suits and ties are required. Are we to believe that basketball is a more important endeavor than representing God Almighty to the world? I know people are just following trends, but when trends fill our pulpits and seats with dishonor, they must be rejected." [5]

Common sense teaches us that what this man says is true. Why is this difficult for so many in the ministry to grasp? We should ask ourselves, "What are we communicating to the world around us when we allow our worship services to become places of casual worship?" This is the heart of the problem when casual dress is permitted or even encouraged for worship. One theologian understood this and said:

"What are we communicating in the way we worship?" Does our worship reflect the glory and character of God and His gospel or the "felt needs" of people? I once heard R. C. Sproul say, "All form is an art form and every art form communicates something." It matters what we do in worship because it reflects what we believe about God." [6]

The Word of God is our final authority in matters of faith and practice. But it is also essential that those who serve the

Lord are able to exercise common sense and apply biblical principles to the existential situations that we face in worship. I repeat what R.C. Sproul says about worship, *"It matters what we do in worship because it reflects what we believe about God."*

4

What Does Cultural Compromise Have To Say About Casual Dress In Worship?

"One does not structure the church to meet the felt needs and desires of the tares. The purpose of corporate assembly, which has its roots in the Old Testament, is for the people of God to come together corporately to offer their sacrifices of praise and worship to God. So the first rule of worship is that it be designed for believers to worship God in a way that pleases God."   R. C. Sproul

The culture we live in today is secular and anti-Christian. By "cultural compromise" I am referring to the practice of bringing the styles and standards of the world into the Church. Robert Murray McCheyne, the great Scottish minister said, *"I looked for the Church and found it in the world. I looked for the world and alas, I found it in the Church."*

Those who dress casually in worship are not being biblical, they are not being creative, they are not being cool, they are not being proper examples to the rest of the church. Those who dress casual are not being a witness to the culture—they have been captured by the culture. Instead of leading the culture to something higher and more glorious, they have been compromised by the fallen and godless culture of the world. Casual worship in style, dress and music reveals a faulty ecclesiology. The church is the center of God's kingdom. When pastors dress casual for Sunday worship, but then dress up for funerals and weddings, they are revealing the hypocrisy of their hearts and their lack of discernment. People dress up for funerals and weddings because those occasions call for a certain amount of respect and decorum. How is it that those same pastors cannot see that throne room worship is even greater in importance than these other occasions?

Once a church starts down the path to casual dress in worship, you have opened the door to pandora's box. From a book on the proper use of music in worship comes this quote:

> "The late Gordon Sears, who had an evangelistic music ministry for many years and ministered with Rudy Atwood, was saddened before his death by the dramatic change that was occurring in many fundamental baptist churches. He warned: 'When the standard of music is lowered, then the standard of dress is also lowered. When the standard of dress is lowered, then the standard of conduct is also lowered." [1]

In a church in Pittsburgh, Pennsylvania that I preached at many years ago, a young man wore a t-shirt that had a picture of a female movie star on his shirt that was sexually provocative, sensual, and suggestive. Not only was I shocked at this, but I was also surprised that there were no leaders in the church who would address this issue. The young man was not a visitor, but a member of the church. The Christian church in the West has compromised with this post-modern culture and has surrendered it's power and purity for cultural relevance.

This trade off has not been beneficial to the overall health of the church.

How do we explain the compromise that so many Christian churches have made with the fallen and unbelieving culture? I believe that the leadership of the church has failed to stay faithful to historical and biblical theology and has gone head over heels for pragmatism. This comment from a Christian theologian verifies what I am saying:

> *"Two enemies have eroded the scriptural foundation of biblical faith in America: liberalism and pragmatism. The old enemy of the early 20th Century was liberalism and it's still with us today. Religious liberalism gave us a "new" or neo-orthodoxy where the Bible was less than God inspired, Christ was less than God, and man was better than we thought. The new enemy in the early 21st Century is pragmatism. I am only slightly facetious when I say that the religious pragmatist of today believes if it puts cushions in the pew, makes people feel better, and generally seems in line with the Bible, it must be of God. Liberals deny the Truth. Pragmatists distort the Truth. While both liberalism and pragmatism are deadly to the gospel, the latter is more subtle and deceptive in that it affirms what the Bible says in word but denies the Scripture in deed."* [2]

Pragmatism is indeed a serious problem facing the church today. Roger N. Niles writes again:

> *"The Bible isn't equally clear on all things regarding worship. Godly judgments by necessity must be made in determining the acceptable way of worshiping God. The question isn't simply "Is this permissible?" The more important question is "Is this proper?" I once heard Dr. J.*

Ligon Duncan III make reference to the fact that "Amazing Grace" could be sung to the tune of "Gilligan's Island." There is nothing in Scripture that prohibits singing "Amazing Grace" to the theme of "Gilligan's Island." But it wouldn't be proper, even for children, because of the serious message of grace communicated so powerfully by that old hymn." [3]

We must not miss what this man says that there is a difference between what is permissible and what is proper. We need spiritual leaders who have the wisdom to know the difference between these two things.

This compromise by the church with the fallen and worldly culture at large is evidenced by the way that many Christian churches seek to give people what they want rather than what they need. This is fueled by the philosophical teaching called "pragmatism." The typical advertising of casual dress—"come as you are to worship God" by many churches reveals the nature of this problem. It's okay to wear cutoffs, shorts, pajamas or just about anything else to church. Or is it? No one doubts that you can worship God while lying in your pajamas in bed, or pray to God while washing dishes in the sink, or lift your heart in adoration and praise while standing in the shower. No one denies this. We are talking about how we dress and act when we are in the house of the Lord on the Lord's Day. Some churches are so compromised with the world that they have turned their services into bar and theatre centers, and some have even turned their Sunday worship into a drive-in theatre style of worship. These things must surely grieve the Holy Spirit.

One pastor relates how he saw a young man who was served communion while wearing a T-shirt that advertised a particular brand of beer. It seems that there is little understanding of holding a high view of worship that does not profane sacred things by things mundane, trivial or irreverent.

The church has compromised with the worldly culture by a number of ways. One pastor writes:

> *"We have allowed society to impose its ideals on us, and they have taught us that everyone and everything should be of equal importance. As a result, things and people that should be revered and honored no longer are, and the things of God, ministers of God, and even God Himself are not treated as special and holy."* [4]

Again, he writes:

> *"In our quest to provide a worship experience that in every way resembles a rock concert, we have kept nothing sacred. People can come right from the nightclub into the church and barely notice a difference. The atmosphere is light and party-like. Entertainment and convenience have replaced anointing and substance. Leaders see the people's enthusiasm and think a move of God is taking place, when really so much of it is just a display of the flesh."* [5]

This is the great compromise of the Christian church. The culture has influenced the church rather than the church influencing the culture. If the current weakness and inability of the church to impact culture tells us anything, it should tell us that our attempts at making our faith casual has not made any significant impact on the world around us. Again, we read:

> *"The Church today has allowed modern culture to pull it into the ditch of extremism in the area of ultra-casual dress and appearance. We should actually be influencing society with our high standards of godliness, but have*

instead taken the lead in embracing all things casual. The holy occasion of worship is profaned when we regard it as common and casual." [6]

The main reason that many pastors are now dressing down in the worship service is that they have a desire to grow the church. The tragedy is that they are making some serious mistakes in their well-intentioned reason for dressing casual in the pulpit. Have they forgotten what the purpose of worship really is? One student of worship commented:

"Ninety percent of the churches in America are under 200 members... And they look around and see that the churches that are flourishing are the ones that we call happy-clappy churches. "What's your felt need?" If it's pop-psychology, we got it. People don't beat on the door saying, "Please can I have expository preaching every Sunday?" [7]

So what do these pastors conclude who are struggling to grow their congregations? They have concluded that the only way to grow their church is to dress down, become more casual and make every effort to entice more sinners to come and be relaxed in the church service. These pastors have forgotten that the purpose of worship is not to build up a bigger audience, but rather it is to build up the people of God who worship there. They have also forgotten that until the Holy Spirit regenerates the sinner he will not have a heart to come into the presence of God. But if we use the world's music, the world's methods, and the world's dress to entice people to come to church who have no interest to do so in the first place, what have we accomplished?

For the most part today, the church is characterized by a worldly spirit of casual and careless Christianity. The glory of God has departed from the sanctuaries of many so-called

Christian churches. The church is feverishly working at being relevant with the world around it, and while it strains to make itself less offensive to non-churched people, it has become irrelevant. Further examples of the compromise of the church with the world is seen by the following comments:

> "...when an immature youth pastor says to impressionable kids "Jesus is an awesome dude" or "Jesus Rocks!" he is not communicating the "I AM". He inadvertently communicates a lesser god even though his intention is to communicate the God of the Bible. The same distortion occurs when the atonement of Christ is reduced to a T-shirt mimicking a beer commercial that says, "This Blood's For You." Another example happened a few years ago when a "Christian" advertising campaign sold T-shirts, bumper stickers, and coffee cups printed with the slogan "Jesus Is My Homeboy." This is not just bad taste and immaturity it's blasphemy. Trivializing the character of the true God communicates another god - a false god." [8]

Not all churches that are dabbling with casual dress in worship have gone as far as the comments revealed by the quote above, but this tends to be the direction that casual worship goes. My fear is that dressing casually is the first step in the wrong direction. Once casual worship embraces a full scaled contemporary approach to the worship of God the following errors begin to emerge:

> "Contemporary Christianity has replaced sanctuaries with family life centers, pulpits with podiums, chancels with stages, formality with informality, sermons with talks, preaching with sharing, discipleship with psychology, congregational singing with special music, words with images, psalms and hymns with praise

choruses, decorum with casualness, sin with dysfunction, bibles and hymnbooks with overheads, choirs and organs with praise teams and bands, corporate worship with individual experience, doctrine with feeling, theology with anthropology, God's glory with man's need etc., etc., ad infinitum ad nauseam. Why? The stated reason is to communicate the gospel to this generation and win souls. But what do these changes actually communicate to people? When you change things that shouldn't be changed or that are, in fact, unchangeable you imply that the God who never changes does change. Consequently, our generation is witnessing a redefinition of biblical faith by Contemporary Christianity, inadvertently for the most part, communicating a different god, a different gospel and a different goal than the Scriptures teach." [9]

The church will thrive, grow, experience the presence of God and find God once again fighting her battles when the Lord's servants feed their flocks what they need instead of feeding them what they want.

Conclusion

"A son honors his father, and a servant his master. If then I am the Father, where is My honor?..."

Malachi 1:6

Are we to despair completely by the compromise of the Lord's servants and by the defection of His people from biblical standards? Reports show that some young people are now going the opposite direction. There is a move in our country among many to return to a more serious form of worship. Many people are moving to the Eastern Orthodox Church or the Roman Catholic Church in their search for a worship experience that is more than trivial and juvenile. There are those who desire a worship service that is more reflective of throne room worship as it takes place in heaven. There is a longing by many today for a more liturgical worship that exalts the transcendence of God and that engages the entire man in worship with all of his senses and feelings. One Christian writes:

> *"It is a lie to believe that I have to be just like the world in order to reach the world. I can be as different from the world as light is from darkness, and if the power of God is allowed to flow, the world will see the light and a percentage of them will run to it. The nice, non-sloppy*

clothes that I wear to magnify and honor my Heavenly Father, and to respect the anointing on my life, will never keep anyone from knowing God. Compromise, lack of honor, and relaxed standards of living will keep many from seeing the light. We've tried to reach people by becoming casual, but misrepresenting God is not the way to reach people. Because the Church looks just like the world, many in the church have gone back to the world – drifting far from the path because God's standards are not on display with clarity and accuracy." [1]

It is encouraging to know that there are many who are now rethinking the whole approach to worship. These students of history and of Scripture are coming to the conclusion that casual worship has been weighed in the balances and found wanting. If this trend continues, there may yet be hope that the Christian church in the West can yet be resurrected and once again be a lively and spiritual force for good. This comment captures the heart of this new movement back to Scripture and to sanity:

"'Contemporary worship' to me is an oxymoron. Biblically, worship is what angels and morning stars did before creation; what Abraham, Moses and the Levites, and the many-tongued Jewish diaspora at Pentecost did. It is what the martyrs, now ascended, do, and what all believers since the apostles have done. More importantly, it is what we will do eternally; worship is essentially (not accidentally) eschatological. And nothing could celebrate the eschatological forever less than something that celebrates the contemporary now. So ultimately, I think the Apostles' Creed will stick its camel's nose into the liturgical tent, and assert again our celebration of the 'holy

Conclusion

catholic church, the communion of the saints.' The sooner the better." [2]

The Christian has a high calling to glorify God in all things. All Christians and especially pastors should consider how they dress, not just at church but at other times as well. Whether we like it or not, our dress is telling a story about our lives and about our faith. One pastor made this observation:

"A Christian must remember that the way a person dresses is a definite indication of what kind of person he or she is. Attire can be an important part of our testimony. Dress for both man or woman should respect the Bible principles of modesty, with ornamentation, non-conformed to the fads and fashions of the world, and express humility and simplicity. A person should ask himself, What does my dress tell others about me? Does it draw attention to me or bring glory to God?" [3]

I have raised the question, *"Does casual dress in our worship services by both the ministers and the laity, enhance or distract from biblical worship?"* In seeking to answer that question, I have made appeals to the Scriptures, tradition, common sense, and cultural compromise. I humbly ask you to pray over what I have said. What does the way you dress at church say about you as a Christian? Does your pastor reflect honor, respect, and serious devotion to God in his decorum in the pulpit on Sundays? Is your church being a witness to the dying and unbelieving culture around it, or is your church conformed to the world? I fear that many pastors and churches are part of the problem rather than being part of the solution.

So what should we all do about this? I do not want anyone to attack, scold or rebuke their pastor. First, if you agree with what I have been saying, then start to set an example yourself by how you and your family dress at church. Second, you can pray for your pastor and church leaders and encourage them to rethink their standards for the worship service. Third, do not treat those who visit your church (who are dressed casually) in an unloving way. Welcome everyone to your church and be gracious to all. Finally, worship God fervently and faithfully on the Lord's Day. Worship the Lord in the beauty of holiness. Let your example shine and your life be a testimony to the grace and the glory of God.

"Let's not allow our local churches to become sanctuaries of the sloppy and temples of the tacky. Let's respect our Master, minister and message." [Dr. Paul Tassell]

Worship for the believer is a spiritual journey into the heavenly places in Christ and draws the Christian into communion with their risen and ascended Lord. Such a spiritual and mysterious ascent into the presence of God should never be casual.

(For a full discussion on the subject of worship, please see my book, *"What The Bible Teaches About Worship"* published by Evangelical Press.)

Footnotes

Introduction

1. Joel Siegel, What Happened To Honor? (Big God Media, 2013), Kindle Edition, Loc, 398-399 of 1962.//
2. John Blake, Stop Dressing So Tacky For Church, October 13, 2014, CNN Belief Blog.
3. R. C. Sproul Jr., From the internet: http://www.ligonier.org/blog/come-you-arent/

Chapter One

1. Thomas F. Booher, Reforming The Reformed's Worship? From the internet: http://tulipdrivenlife.blogspot.com/2016/05/reforming-reformeds-worship.html
2. Janet Treadway, What Your Appearance Says About You.

Chapter Two

1. thebible.net, From The Internet: http://thebible.net/introchurch/ch49.html
2. R. C. Sproul, From The Internet: http://www.ligonier.org/learn/devotionals/role-tradition/
3. G. K. Chesterton, On Democracy and Modernity, Free Thinker Blog, Nov. 14, 2007.

4. Jason Helopoulos, Casual Worship, TGC, Guest blogger, August 23, 2012.

5. Frank Sonnenberg, From the internet: http://www.franksonnenbergonline.com/blog/7-reasons-why-traditions-are-so-important/

6. Leonard R. Payton, CONGREGATIONAL SINGING AND THE MINISTRY OF THE WORD

Chapter Three

1. Webster's New World Dictionary, Second College Edition.

2. John Blake, Stop Dressing So Tacky For Church, October 13, 2014, CNN Belief Blog.

3. The Wittenberg Door, From the internet: http://wittenberg-door.blogspot.com/2010/12/dressing-for-worship.html

4. Joel Siegel, What Happened To Honor? (Big God Media, 2013), Kindle Edition, Loc, 346-399 of 1962.

5. Ibid, loc. 370-376.

6. Dr. Mark Creech, What We Wear To Church, Does It Matter? Christian Post Columnist, September 9, 2014.

Chapter Four

1. Gordon Sears, quoted in a book on music wars in the church.

2. Roger N.Wiles, Style and Substance: Are Traditional, Contemporary, and Blended Legitimate Categories of Worship?

3. Ibid.

4. Joel Siegel, What Happened To Honor? (Big God Media, 2013), Kindle Edition, Loc, 305 of 1962.

5. Ibid, loc, 310

6. Ibid, loc, 340

7. From the internet: http://www.christianbookpreviews.com/christian-book-author-interview.php?isbn=1567690769

8. Roger N.Wiles, Style and Substance: Are Traditional, Contemporary, and Blended Legitimate Categories of Worship?

9. Ibid.

Conclusion

1. Joel Siegel, What Happened To Honor? (Big God Media, 2013), Kindle Edition, Loc, 446 of 1962.

2. T. David Gordan, The Imminent Decline of Contemporary Worship Music: Eight Reasons.

3. From the Internet: The Christian's Appearance, www.bibleviews.com/Dress.html

www.ingramcontent.com/pod-product-compliance
Lightning Source LLC
Chambersburg PA
CBHW031450070426
42452CB00037B/437